ARIZONA 101

An Irreverent Short Course for New Arrivals

By James E. Cook

Sketches by Lee Wells

Other books by James E. Cook
  Dry Humor: Tales of Arizona Weather
  The Arizona Trivia Book
  Arizona Landmarks
  Arizona Pathways
  Travel Arizona: The Backroads (co-author)
  Discovered Treasures

Third Edition, revised
Copyright © 1997 James E. Cook

Published by: Gem Guides Book Co.
              315 Cloverleaf Drive, Suite F
              Baldwin Park, CA 91706

Library of Congress Catalog Number: 96-78396
ISBN 0-935182-80-2

Cover Illustration: Lee Wells
Cover Design: Kimura-Bingham Graphic Design, Tucson, AZ

Printed in the United States of America.

TABLE OF CONTENTS

For Susan, who hotwires my synaptic gaps and makes me feel young.

1 - THAT BIG, EMPTY MAP

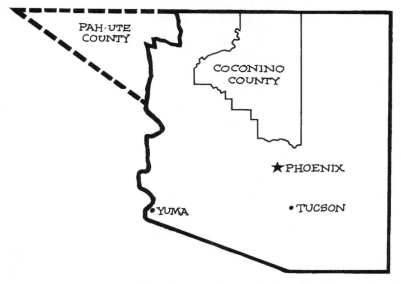

So you've turned in the rental truck, or sent the moving van away. Suddenly you feel alone.

What have you done? Why are you in this peculiar place called Arizona?

Can you find your way to your new job? Why are all the locals wearing jackets, while you feel like sunning yourself by the pool? Will they think you're odd?

Or maybe you're just visiting, trying to figure out why your in-laws and so many others decided to moved to this warm, dry place with the unfamiliar vegetation, or lack thereof.

Perhaps a talkative old-timer (who moved here two years ago from Wheeling, West Virginia) is telling you scare stories about scorpions, taxes and how hot it gets in the summer.

Don't panic. About three thousand people a week move into Arizona from out of state. The shock of relocation has not actually killed anyone.

Arizona 101 is a short course to help you feel at home. Its author is an adult native of Arizona who specializes in writing about the state, because he doesn't know much about anything else. He is proud he had the good sense to be born in a state to which so many easterners and midwesterners decided to move. Through the eyes of these late-comers, he has learned to appreciate one of the most splendidly varied states among the fifty.

Read this book and you'll soon look Arizona, talk Arizona, and be able to share inside jokes with the rest of us.

So where are we, geographically speaking? Arizona starts at 109 degrees, 2 minutes and 59 seconds west longitude and proceeds in a westerly direction. Four Corners, the only place in the nation common to four states, is Arizona's northeastern corner.

Depending on where you land in Arizona, you are about 2,400 miles west of New York City and 1,700 miles west of Chicago. Arizona is 335 miles wide and 390 miles long, with a net area of 113,909 square miles after subtracting the jogs in its boundaries.

Arizona used to be larger. On a map, extend the Arizona-Utah border westward to where it would intersect the California-Nevada border. The wedge-shaped point of Nevada used to be Pah-Ute County, Arizona Territory. But in 1866, Congress gratuitously gave Pah-Ute to Nevada, which eventually would need a place to build Las Vegas. Some Arizonans still mourn "the lost county of Pah-Ute."

Others never heard of it.

As it was, Arizona ended up bigger than New Zealand. One county, Coconino (second largest county in the U.S.) is as large as New Hampshire, New Jersey and Delaware combined, with fifty-two miles left over for a swap meet.

If you compare the Arizona map with that of the state you came from, you may wonder if Rand McNally printed Arizona during an ink shortage. Yes, Arizona is really that empty. While it is the sixth largest state in land area, it ranks twenty-fourth in population. There are only 35 people per square mile, compared to 366 in the state of New York.

Another reason for Arizona's unlined face: It is, believe it or not, one of the most urbanized states in the nation. More than fifty-eight percent of Arizonans live in Maricopa County, the Phoenix metropolitan area. Another eighteen percent live in the Tucson area. Concentrating people in urban areas has allowed us to keep the rest of the state open to panoramic views and breathtaking *Arizona Highways* sunsets.

You may think of Arizona as desolate desert. To be sure, there are vast areas where the supply of distance exceeds the demand. Comedian Mark Russell once likened one of our congressional districts to 200,000 square miles of kitty litter.

But the desert is a lot more interesting than you think; many learn to love it. And for variety, it's never far to a mountain or a lake or one of our splendid canyons, carved by the streams which flow through them.

Here are some miscellaneous facts to get you started feeling like an Arizonan:

• The highest point in Arizona is Humphreys Peak, 12,643 feet, north of Flagstaff. The lowest point is seventy feet where the Colorado River flows into Mexico south of Yuma.

• Arizona has only fifteen counties, compared to ninety-two in Indiana.

• The highest temperature ever recorded in Arizona was a mere 129 degrees Fahrenheit at Lake Havasu City in 1994. The maximum at Phoenix was 122.

• Arizona has dozens of man-made lakes, and you'll hear it said that per capita boat ownership is the highest in the nation. That is absurd. Arizona ranks somewhere near the middle of the fifty states in boat ownership.

• Arizona's state bird is the cactus wren, and the state tree is the palo verde. The official state neckwear, believe it or not, is the bola tie.

• You will hear of "the Grand Canyon of the Colorado," referring not to the state of Colorado, but to the river which dug the Canyon. The Canyon is entirely within Arizona.

• The Arizona Strip is not a dirty dance or a special cut of steak; it is that portion of the state lying between the Colorado River and Utah.

• Do not be surprised if you aren't greeted warmly when you complain, "They don't do it this way back in Illinois (or whatever state you came from)."

• There are presently no active volcanoes in Arizona.

2 - A SUDDEN LOOK AT A LONG PAST

Many Arizona towns, including Phoenix, celebrated centennials in the last quarter-century. That might lead you to believe the state has a short history.

Wrong. Tucson was founded as a Spanish presidio in 1775, the year colonists in the East rebelled against the British. Another town, the Hopi Indian pueblo Oraibi, has been continuously inhabited since 1050 A.D. Here's a crash course on how we got the way we are.

First there were the Native Americans, who began coming over from Asia thousands of years ago. The latest to arrive were the Apache and Navajo, who came into the Southwest about the time the first Spanish explorers came north from Mexico in 1539.

By that time, native cultures had developed, thrived and been canceled by drought, disease or other raiding Indians. A number of cultures "vanished" between 1,200 and 1,500 A.D., abandoning condo-like pueblo condos in the caves of central and northern Arizona.

In the south, the advanced Hohokam disappeared before the arrival of Columbus, leaving behind ruins of high-density housing and a complex system of irrigation canals. (The natives did not actually disappear; no one put their pictures on milk cartons or junk mail. Anthropologists are pretty sure they evolved into today's tribes, but they can't bridge that gap in the record, and it drives them crazy. (Some of us think the Hohokam went to San Diego for the summer and never came back.)

Spanish soldiers and missionaries began exploring Arizona in 1539. They introduced cattle ranching and Catholicism to the Tohono O'odham and Pima peoples of southern Arizona. Pueblo people in the north weren't so friendly. On July 4, 1776, restless Franciscan friar Francisco Garces wrote in his journal of being evicted from Oraibi by Hopis who wanted no part of Catholicism.

That same year, Captain Juan Bautista de Anza set out from the Spanish presidio at Tubac (founded in 1752) to lead an expedition that would found the city of San Francisco.

Mexicans ejected the Spaniards, and from 1821 to 1848 Arizona belonged to Mexico. The Hispanic population during this time probably did not exceed one thousand people.

Meanwhile U.S. mountain men, trespassing on Mexican territory, began exploring the region's waterways in 1826. General Stephen Watts Kearny's Army of the West followed the Gila to California in 1846 to help conquer Mexican California.

At the end of the Mexican War in 1848, the Treaty of Guadalupe Hidalgo gave the United States that part of Arizona north of the Gila River, where there was not a single Anglo-American settlement. During the 1850s, several government exploring parties, seeking wagon and railroad routes along the thirty-fifth parallel, traversed northern Arizona. One party used camels as beasts of burden, adding a colorful chapter of Arizona lore (see Chapter 12).

The Gadsden Purchase of 1854 acquired southern Arizona

from Mexico. The purchase was the work of southern senators, who foresaw a break with the north over slavery and wanted a southern railroad route to the Pacific.

At first, Arizona was part of New Mexico Territory. When the name Arizona was used, it usually referred to the part of New Mexico south of the Gila and west of the Rio Grande. The name came from Real de Arissona, a rich silver mining district in Sonora, southwest of present-day Nogales, Arizona.

In 1862 the Confederacy proclaimed Confederate Arizona to be the southern half of New Mexico Territory, from Texas to California. Fewer than one hundred Confederate soldiers under Captain Sherod Hunter occupied Tucson and environs, but the Union's California Volunteers soon drove them out.

In 1863, President Abraham Lincoln divided New Mexico north and south and created the territory of Arizona. Because Tucson was a hotbed of Confederate sympathies, the first capital was Prescott, a booming gold camp in the Bradshaw Mountains. Members of the governing party sent west in 1863 indicated by their letters home that they were more interested in finding gold than in civic betterment. But then, that was the magnet that drew most adventurers here.

Native Americans did not stand idly by while easterners took over their land. The natives fought for thirty years to hold their land. U.S. military forces, skeletal before the Civil War, returned in force afterward to protect the gold and silver mines, farms and cattle ranches, and to subjugate the Indians. Sadly, many of the white settlers favored exterminating the natives.

Soldiers were stationed at Fort McDowell on the Verde River to protect the road from Tucson to Prescott, and the road to the mining boom town of Wickenberg. They needed hay for their horses; new settlers needed grain and vegetables. Farmers began digging out old Hohokam irrigation canals along the Salt River.

Soldier of fortune, Jack Swilling, formed an irrigation company to put in new canals and ditches in the area that would become Phoenix. That was in 1867; there were about three hundred residents by the time Phoenix town site was laid out in 1870.

By the mid-1880s, two transcontinental railroads crossed Arizona, the Southern Pacific in the south and the Santa Fe in the north. The capital was moved from Prescott to Tucson, back to Prescott and finally, in 1889, to growing Phoenix.

Farmers in the Salt River Valley were sometimes exhausting the undependable waters of the Salt, which fluctuated from drought to flood stage. A large storage dam was needed. After the Federal Reclamation Act became law in 1902, Roosevelt Dam was built northeast of Phoenix, the first of a series of dams on the Salt and Verde Rivers that brought stability and prosperity to the valley.

Statehood was a little harder to achieve, partly because of lawlessness which had prevailed in Arizona late in the nineteenth century. Finally, on Valentine's Day, 1912, Arizona became the forty-eighth state. Gold and silver mines had pretty much run their course, but electrification of eastern cities created a new demand for copper. Arizona had plenty of that underneath its rugged mountains; the copper industry still thrives.

Until the 1940s, Arizona's growth was relatively predictable. During World War II, the fair-weather state became the site of dozens of military training bases. Aggressive business promoters made sure the military knew that Arizona's weather made it a good place to build air bases and ground training facilities.

Arizona never was the same again. Many GIs who first saw the state as trainees returned to live as soon as they could. The word spread: Evaporative coolers and air conditioning had made it possible to live on the desert in comfort, even in summer.

Population growth became an accepted part of life. The rest, as they say, is history. There are many good books available on the colorful facets of Arizona's past, which goes back a bit farther than most people think.

3 - YOU ARE NOT DAVY CROCKETT

Two major phenomena shape much of the conversation in Arizona: weather, and the population growth which fair weather triggered. A bank statistician has said of the mushrooming population: "How do I count thee? Let me love the ways."

Nature lovers and environmentalists aren't so happy.

Perhaps coming to Arizona is your big adventure, your break with the past. We're glad you feel that way, but you are not a lone pioneer facing the wilderness.

In 1940, there were fewer than half a million people in Arizona. By 1996, there were more than four million residents, and more coming every day. Between 1980 and 1996, the state added 1,520,000 people.

Much of the growth, of course, was in the Phoenix area. Phoenix and its older satellite cities, once connected only by farm roads, have grown toward each other and become a patchwork of contiguous cities, distinguishable only by the color schemes of their police cars.

Since 1940, Phoenix has grown from a town of 64,000 people to the nation's seventh largest municipality, with more than a million residents. Its land area grew from 17 to 469 square miles, larger than the land base of Los Angeles, as subdivisions leapfrogged and gobbled up former farmland and some raw desert. It might be larger, but its satellite cities also annexed large areas, hemming Phoenix in. Like other western cities that developed in partnership with the automobile, the metropolis has sprawled across an area as large as the Los Angeles Basin.

The growth was not all confined to the Phoenix area. One example of what happened: At the gates of Fort Huachuca in southern Arizona, there used to be a hamlet known as Fry. That is now the location of Sierra Vista, Arizona's thirteenth largest city, with more than 37,850 people. Several other new communities near the fort have a combined population greater than that of Sierra Vista.

Brand new communities have popped up with amazing regularity. Lake Havasu City, home of the transplanted London Bridge, was a remote World War II recreation site for Army Air Corps trainees.

Prescott Valley, which didn't exist thirty years ago, has a population of 16,043. Upscale Carefree rose out of the boulders and brushy desert north of the winter resort town of Scottsdale. Not far away is Fountain Hills, a city that didn't exist a few years back. Del Webb's Sun City and Sun City West added sixty thousand new people. Webb is now building a third Sun City, and planning yet another community of fifty thousand people north of Phoenix.

Green Valley, south of Tucson, has become a magnet for newcomers. Several summer satellites of Flagstaff have become year-round towns. This is by no means a complete list of new towns.

There has been considerable anguish about whether a state ought to be allowed to grow so rapidly. Urbanization, and the resulting hordes fanning out to explore Arizona's wilderness, are eroding many values that brought people here. Natives cringe. Newcomers think the borders should have been closed immediately after their arrival—a sentiment that dates back to Geronimo.

But Arizona likes to think it is a freewheeling bastion of free enterprise. The prevailing attitude is that every American has a right to live where he wants, and that real estate developers have a right to make a killing.

Thus there has never been a determined effort to limit Arizona's population growth. As you explore the community you're living in, mark its perimeters in your mind. Take notes or photos, if you wish. Go back a year from now and see how the place has grown. By that time you'll be a genuine old-timer.

4 - DON'T BE SNOWED ABOUT WEATHER

There's no hiding the fact that the climate which makes desert Arizona so attractive in winter causes some terribly hot summers. The summer weather has been called a "dry heat," and there is some truth in that.

However, it soon becomes apparent to the newcomer that what occurs in Arizona in the summer is a *hot* heat. Every old-timer will be happy to tell you where he was the day President John F. Kennedy was assassinated, and how hot it was the day he saw his first evaporative cooler. (Readers who want more detail should consult the author's authoritative *Dry Humor: Tales of Arizona Weather,* also published by Gem Guides Book Co.).

For the record, the highest temperature ever recorded in

Arizona was 129 degrees, reported at Lake Havasu City in 1994. For many years, the record maximum at Phoenix was 118 degrees. But on June 25, 1990, the thermometer climbed to 120 degrees; the following afternoon it hit 122. Sundials in the Salt River Valley ran an hour fast. The high at Tucson that day was a more moderate 117.

The temperature of the ambient air is measured in the shade five feet above the ground. It gets much hotter on unshaded paving, vinyl upholstery and in closed automobiles. Never leave metal tools lying in the sun.

In an average year in Phoenix, there are eight days when the temperature reaches 110 degrees or higher; in a really hot year, however, it's possible to see several days that top out near 115.

Long-time Phoenix climatologist Robert J. Schmidli wrote, "Most residents of Phoenix put up with temperatures below 110 without grumbling. However, when the mercury climbs to 110 or higher, even old-timers feel the heat and begin to complain."

The sun shines eighty-six percent of the possible daylight hours in Phoenix and Tucson, and ninety-one percent in Yuma. That's enough sunlight to drive people mad. Natives pray for rain (see following chapter).

The driest year on record was 1956. At Davis Dam on the Colorado River, .07 inch of rain was reported the entire year. Phoenix, which averages 7.05 inches of rainfall annually, had only 2.82 inches of rainfall in 1956.

While desert towns engage in a silly competition to see which can report the nation's highest temperature on any given day, other places in Arizona's mountains frequently report the nation's lowest temperature.

Arizona has some of the most varied geography in the nation, ranging from 70 feet elevation to 12,643 feet. If all of Arizona's mountains were ironed out flat, the state would be as large as Texas, and just about as interesting. (The author's maternal grandfather was born in Flat, Texas, which may explain why he came to Arizona.)

The greatest snowfall reported in one season was 400.9 inches measured at Sunrise Mountain in the winter of 1972-1973. The coldest temperature reported in the state was -40 Fahrenheit at Hawley Lake in 1971. Hawley Lake also had the wettest year recorded for any place in Arizona in 1978, when precipitation totaled 58.92 inches. Wooden signposts took root.

Then there's Workman Creek, about thirty miles northnorthwest of Globe. On October 4 and 5, 1970, it rained 11.40 inches in twenty-four hours. Many Arizonans remember the devastating floods that killed twenty-three people over that Labor Day weekend.

They also remember the big storm(s) of 1967-1968. Snow stacked up to ninety-one inches at Hawley Lake, the greatest depth on record for any settled location in Arizona. The sixty-seven inches that fell at Heber Ranger Station December 13-16, 1967, was the heaviest recorded snowfall in one storm.

It has snowed in Phoenix, too. It snowed one inch in January, 1933, and another inch in January, 1937. There have been lesser amounts since, but don't bother to bring your snow tires, unless you're moving to Flagstaff.

You will often hear exaggerated accounts of Arizona winds. The record wind was a gust that peaked at eighty-six miles per hour at Phoenix on July 7, 1976. The record for persistent wind is held by Winslow, where the wind seldom stops. It is the only National Weather Service station in Arizona where the rain gauge is mounted horizontally.

5 – OUR DELIGHTFUL STORMS

As a 727 leaves Kennedy or O'Hare on a February morning, bound for Phoenix, the captain comes on the inter-calm and dispenses tranquillity to the passengers: "You'll be happy to know that the temperature in Phoenix is seventy-two degrees and the sun is shining."

Good weather is the main reason so many people come to Arizona. But there is a less benign side to Arizona weather, and you need to be prepared.

It does rain here. When everyone at work rushes to the windows, you know it's raining—if your building has windows. Many buildings are built without windows because it's cheaper to air condition such a structure.

Sometimes it rains a lot. The desert soil, with little vegetation to keep it loose, is about as absorbent as Saran Wrap. Water flows toward the low spots, and begins to accumulate in desert washes, and in streets.

Many streets in the Phoenix and Tucson areas dip through low washes. Construction of bridges and storm drains has not kept up with population growth. New lakes form in low-lying streets. Motorists drown their engines. A car with a tight bottom, like an older Volkswagen, will plane for a block or two before it sinks.

Traffic slows. Radio stations broadcast lists of street closures, but they can't keep up with them all.

Wet pavement is hazardous, because a film of petroleum residue builds up during the long dry spells. Add a little water and you have lubricated streets, as slick as black ice. Windshield wipers dry out between rains, and scrape futilely across filmy glass during a storm.

Arizona residents, accustomed to dry streets and unlimited visibility, don't know how to drive in the rain. They become overcautious and get in the way of recent arrivals from the Northeast, who like an opportunity to show off their driving skills. Mix in a few winter visitors and over-cautious retirees, then dial 911.

These things can happen as a result of a simple winter storm from the Pacific. If rain persists, or if a winter rain falls on top of a snowpack in the mountains, water rushes to the low spots, i.e. the bed of the Salt River, where it spills over onto flood plains. Much of the Phoenix metropolitan area was built on flood plains. During long dry cycles, people forget about floods. Newcomers never knew. Lives are ruined, and sometimes people die.

The Salt River, normally dry as it passes through Phoenix, now resembles the Nile or the Missouri in flood. Dry-weather road crossings of the Salt are washed on down to the Gila River, and eventually to the Gulf of California.

The Salt divides the metropolitan area, and motorists are confined to a handful of bridges, which occasionally wash away during the floods.

Tucson has a similar situation, for the Santa Cruz River flows through the city; so does one of its major tributaries, Rillito Creek. Tucsonans jest that on the first day the temperature reaches one hundred degrees, the ice breaks up the Santa Cruz, opening it to navigation.

The real joke is that the Santa Cruz is always bone dry, except when it's flooding. Winter visitors to both cities who came here to play golf and shuffleboard, have to hang out at the shopping malls. But they are treated to a rare sight—water in our rivers. They also get to see the rare "one-hundred-year flood," calculated to occur once every century. Sometimes we have two or three a year. Disruption is not limited to the metropolitan areas, of course. Little of Arizona was designed to contain water.

Summer storms, spun by a monsoon blowing off the Gulf of California, are even more abrupt and sometimes violent. Videotape of people fighting for their homes and their lives goes out on national TV to a disbelieving audience which thinks Arizona is all sunny golf courses and singing cowboys.

In summer, thunderheads grow tall and their tops change from silvery white to dark gray and black. At ground level, the air becomes still and eerie. Suddenly, it is as though Jehovah had tripped a trap door and let a storm whoosh out of the bottoms of the clouds.

Sometimes the impending storm creates legendary dust

storms, towering curtains of dirt, twigs and small reptiles scooped up from desert and farm land and sifted onto the cities in the path of the storm. Dust and debris are deposited on windows, clean cars and in residential swimming pools. Dust storms sweeping across freeways have caused several deadly chain collisions.

Sometimes tornadoes and lesser funnel clouds dispatch roofs to new addresses, and turn aluminum-skinned mobile homes into metal sculpture.

Lightning is hot and very ominous against dark clouds and darker mountains. Then the rain begins, big drops at first, followed by torrents. If the rain lasts for long, it's back to Flood City.

If the storm is brief, it's back to Arizona's usually sunny weather—boring but pleasant.

6 – A PRONOUNCED DIFFERENCE IN WORDS

There are more "Hs" in the spoken language of Arizona than show up in print, a result of the Hispanic influence that created a tongue called "Spanglish."

"Gs" and "Js" usually sound like Hs in Spanish. Thus the word "Gila" is pronounced *"Hee-*la." That poisonous beaded lizard you have heard so much about is called a *"Hee-*la" Monster. The Gila River is one of Arizona's major rivers. It would be incorrect to say the Gila runs across Arizona, because the Gila rarely has water in it.

There also is a Gila County and a town called Gila Bend, sometimes one of the hottest places in the nation.

Many Arizona names are Spanish, or Spanish corruptions of Indian words, or Anglo corruptions of what the Spanish thought the Indians said. The phonetic pronunciations in this chapter are conversational, not scholarly.

Arizonans do not pronounce all Spanish names correctly. Nor do we uniformly mispronounce them as is the custom in Texas, where the historic town of San Jacinto (Sahn Ha-seen-toe) is commonly called "San Juh-*sin*-toe." Mesa, Arizona's third largest city, is pronounced "*May*-suh," close to proper Spanish.

Let's return to the mysterious "H." It occurs in the name of the town of Ajo, pronounced "*Ah*-hoe." The "J" in Navajo is an "H," (Navajo is sometimes misspelled "Navaho.") Mojave (Moe-*hah*-vay), as in the California desert, has been anglicized to Mohave County, Arizona. Javelina (hah-vuh-*lee*-nah) is an ugly wild pig common to Arizona, known for the way it causes hunters to lie.

In combination with "U," the natural "H" becomes a "W." Huatch out for Fort Huachuca (wah-*chuke*-uh), Hualapai (*wa*-luh-pie) and Chiricahua (cheer-uh-*kah*-wuh). Saguaro, sometimes spelled with an "H" instead of a "G," is pronounced "suh-*war*-oh."

The broad Spanish "A" should properly be pronounced "ah," but "uh" is acceptable.

The mining town San Manuel (Sahn mahn-*well*) sounds like "Salmon Wells," and the Phoenix suburb El Mirage sounds like "Elmer Odge." Perhaps the most violence is done to Casa Grande ("big house," named for nearby Hohokam ruins). Most people who live in the small city properly call it *"Cah-sah Grahn*-day." But many Arizonans pronounce it "Cass-uh *Grand"* or worse yet, "Cass-uh *Gran*-dee."

Verde, as in the Verde River, Camp Verde and chili verde, means green. Properly pronounced *"vair*-day," in Spanish, it usually rhymes with "dirty" in Spanglish. Just don't call it "vird."

You may sometimes hear a disk jockey or a TV weatherman talk about the "Mongolian Rim" or the "Magolin" plateau. The Mogollon Rim is an escarpment along a fault line that extends west-northwest from the Arizona-New Mexico border to northwestern Arizona. Don't ask whose fault it is; it was probably named for Juan Ignacio Flores Mogollon, Spanish governor of New Mexico from 1712 to 1715. The governor probably pronounced it "Mogo-yown," but Yanqui tongues have made it "Muggy-*own,"* which rhymes with "funny bone." It is not "muggy-*yawn"* a favorite of TV weathermen.

We mentioned Hualapai, the name of a Native American tribe. Arizona has more pies than a truck stop menu: Yavapai *(Ya*-vuh-pie), a county and a tribe; Pah Ute (Pie-*ute)*, a tribe; and Havasupai (Hav-ah-*sue*-pie), a Native American tribe that lives in Supai (*Sue*-pie) Village.

Canyon de Chelly does not rhyme with belly. It's "Day *shay"* the Chelly being a Spanish assault on the Navajo word "Tsegi," meaning rock. The Spanish preposition "de," meaning "of," is pronounced "day," "de" and "duh" in Arizona.

A couple of other frequently-used Spanish names: "calle," (*"cah*-yay" or *"cah*-yuh") means street, and "ocotillo" ("oh-coe-*tee*-yo" or "oh-coe-*tee*-yuh") is a thorny shrub with gorgeous blooms.

Finally, a few localized, non-Spanish peculiarities: Prescott is pronounced *"Press*-cut," not *"Press*-cot;" Miami is pronounced "My-*am*-uh;" and Tempe is pronounced "Tem-*pee*," not "*Temp*-ee."

7 - WHAT AIR YOU TALKING ABOUT?

Except for a few Spanish and Indian words, Arizonans talk much like everyone else. Arizonans *are* everyone else. They have come from all over the world, and their accents tend to be ground smooth as they talk to each other. The state has no regional dialect, with the exception of the Utah accent found in some areas with a high Mormon population.

The basic English that you bring with you will allow you to

communicate. If you're from Boston, you may be embarrassed to find you are saying "Forgive us our trespasses" while the rest of the congregation is still on "our daily bread." You'll slow down in time.

While the language is the same, some words have different meanings:

AIR: This word has all the usual applications, plus a few local meanings. "Dirty air" refers to the fact that Arizona, once a healing refuge for those who suffered respiratory problems, now tolerates considerable air pollution, both locally generated and imported from California.

More commonly, "air" refers to refrigerated air conditioning. For instance in May someone asks: "Have you turned on the air (at your house) yet?"

Or, while riding in an automobile: "It will only take a few miles for the air to cool the car down."

BANK: 1. That part of an irrigation canal which is supposed to keep the water out of your yard. 2. Any of several thousand branches of financial institutions owned by out-of-state holding companies; placed at ninety-second intervals in urban areas, equipped with drive-through windows and automatic teller machines.

BARBECUE: 1. A ritual, ceremonial feast served to celebrate political campaigns, national holidays, ribbon-cuttings, groundbreakings, cattle sales, rodeos, graduations, bankruptcy auctions, weddings and divorces. 2. A method of cooking meat to be served at the above festivities.

CANAL: Carries irrigation water from reservoir to farm. These are major landmarks in the Phoenix area. A knowledge of where the canals go, and which streets they intercept, will sometimes save you driving three miles out of your way to

35

find a given address.

GRASS: 1. Lawn covering used to disguise the fact that this is a desert. 2. Cannabis. 3. Whatever kind of vegetation beef cattle will eat.

WASH: Usually a broad, shallow water course. It is difficult to tell some of the larger washes from dormant rivers; in places they are the same. A wash is a relative of the ravine, the arroyo, the gully, the gulch and the draw.

LAKE: 1. A body of water impounded by damming a river, creek, wash, arroyo, gully, gulch or draw. 2. Any low spot that once had water in it, and may yet again have water in it. 3. An artificial pond built as an amenity to help sell houses in a sub-division.

FOREST: Any of the eleven and a half million acres of Arizona under the jurisdiction of the U.S. Forest Service, Department of Agriculture. Lower regions of this terrain rarely resemble what we normally think of as forests. You can't see the forest for the rocks. However, the federal government has no Department of Rocks.

WOODS: Any forest which features coniferous trees; surprisingly, there are several million acres of real woods in Arizona.

DIP: 1. Affectionate term for brother-in-law. 2. A low spot where a highway crosses a draw, gully, wash, gulch or arroyo. These are marked by road signs, and it is usually wise to slow down for these, especially during inclement weather. The man you see waist-deep in floodwaters may be standing atop his pickup truck.

PINTO: 1. A kind of bean used in both Mexican food and at barbecues. 2. A color of horse. 3. A rural Democrat, whose leanings may be more Republican that those of urban Republicans.

RIVER: Many Arizona rivers have become largely ceremonial. They have been dammed in the canyons upstream; something about an undammed river makes long-time Arizonans nervous. Dams leave miles of dry river bed downstream, an excellent source of sand and gravel for construction. In wet years, the rivers provide a channel for flood water on its lonely journey to the sea.

Some rivers never had water, except when it rained. A precocious eight-year-old saw a bridge sign that said "New River" and asked, "You mean they're going to put a river there?"

Curiously, rivers with colors in their names usually have water in them: the Colorado and the Verde (Spanish for red and green, respectively); Blue River; and Black River and White River, which join to form not the Grey River, but the Salt.

CREEK: Usually smaller than a river, but more likely to have water in it.

BRONCO: 1. An unruly horse. 2. An all-terrain vehicle sold by Ford.

GARAGE: 1. A place to get automobiles repaired. 2. Additional storage space in many urban homes.

8 - ELEVATION
MOUNTS UP

LEE WELLS

Early in the morning, a family of tourists going to or from
Disneyland emerges stiffly from an automobile at a Flagstaff
gas station. They last saw daylight on the flats of New Mexico,
or the desert freeways across California. Now they find themselves among pine trees, with Arizona's tallest peaks towering
on the horizon.

"Gee, where are we?"

"Really. I thought Arizona was desert."

"Mom, I'm cold!"

It is one of our favorite tricks to play on tourists. Arizona has plenty of the relatively barren desert tourists expect, and a fair area of carved sandstone spires they saw in old John Ford/John Wayne movies.

However, anyone who has been here any time at all will tell you Arizona wouldn't amount to a hill of beans without its abrupt, rugged mountains. The state's mean elevation is four thousand feet. Some of Arizona's lesser mountains dwarf the mountains of New England; in other parts of the country, Arizona's mountains might be national parks. Some of our more substantial towns are around seven thousand feet elevation, and a few hamlets are at eight thousand feet.

Phoenix wears several of its mountains, such as Camelback Mountain and Squaw Peak, inside the city limits. Phoenix South Mountain Park is the largest city park in the nation.

Farther out, there are benign, forested ranges where the whole family can play. And there are some truly mean desert mountain ranges that only a fugitive from justice or a crazed prospector would love.

Here are some of the major prominences:

MOGOLLON RIM: This is not strictly a mountain range, but it comes to mind when you mention "mountains" to an Arizonan. The Rim runs across Arizona's midsection, beginning at the New Mexico border and angling northwest to the area of Lake Mead.

Sometimes the escarpment is not visible, but through some

of the prettiest parts of Arizona, it forms a two-thousand-foot cliff separating two of Arizona's forested areas. Zane Grey had a home in the heavily forested pine country below the Rim, and several of his novels were set there. The basin below is a favorite recreation and summer home area.

Above the Rim, the Coconino Plateau is cut by a grid of steep canyons, well known to dedicated trout fishermen. The plateau gradually slopes downward to the high desert of the Navajo Indian Reservation.

SAN FRANCISCO PEAKS: These beautiful peaks, immediately north of Flagstaff, include Mount Humphreys, tallest in Arizona (12,643 feet). Originally there was one huge volcanic peak. A second eruption blew the top off and left the five existing peaks. (There are more than four hundred volcanic cones in the Flagstaff area.) The mountains have religious significance to both the Navajo and Hopi Indians. The peaks also offer good hiking and skiing, but the fishing is terrible; there are few live streams near the peaks.

WHITE MOUNTAINS: This range, north of the Mogollon Rim in eastern Arizona, is the favorite retreat of many Phoenix and Tucson residents. The mountains are not white at all, except when they are covered in snow.

A lot of amusements are available in this forested range. The favorites seem to be fishing from many lakes and streams, camping and just hiding out. The ports of entry to the White Mountains, Show Low and Springerville, are at an elevation of nearly seven thousand feet. The mountains rise to 11,590 feet at the top of Mount Baldy.

SUPERSTITION MOUNTAINS: This might be called the Kellogg Range, for the flakes who congregate in the west end. The forbidding Superstitions, which rise abruptly from the desert east of Phoenix, are supposedly the site of the fabled

Lost Dutchman Gold Mine, a magnet for gold hunters of every stripe.

A hike or horseback ride quickly puts you out of touch with civilization—and winter visitors who flock into the east end of the Salt River Valley each year. For those who know how to cope with wilderness, the Superstitions are paradise. Those who don't know can quickly get into life-threatening situations (that's true in many of Arizona's mountains). If you don't want to become notorious on the evening news, know where you're going and learn what you're doing.

BRADSHAW MOUNTAINS: These mountains, north of Phoenix and west of Interstate 17, were named for William C. Bradshaw, a prospector who found gold here in the 1860s. Bradshaw took his own life by cutting his throat with a draw knife, but the Bradshaws don't effect most people that way.

Arizona's first Territorial Capital was established at the gold mining boom town of Prescott in 1864. The mountains were thick with gold and silver mines, but many of the boomtowns are ghost towns now. One town that didn't die is the hamlet of Crown King, reached by a rugged, twisting dirt road.

DESERT ISLANDS: Some poet applied this name to isolated mountains, mostly in southern Arizona, that rise almost vertically from the desert floor. Two of the more conspicuous are the Santa Catalinas, which tower over Tucson, and the Santa Ritas south of Tucson.

Others are the Huachucas on the border near Mexico; the Pinalenos (including 10,713-foot Mount Graham) south of Safford; and the gorgeous Chiricahuas, from which Cochise and Geronimo used to hole up between raids on early Anglo arrivals.

MAZATZALS: The long, skinny range lies between Phoenix and Payson, and the first thing you need to know is that the name is commonly mispronounced "Matazals." This range includes dramatic Four Peaks, four distinct prominences that look pretty from Phoenix when they're capped with snow.

Many other ranges have picturesque names: the Growlers, the Tortillas, the Cerbats, the Mules, the Whetsones, the Chocolates. The spire called Picacho Peak between Phoenix and Tucson is redundant; "picacho" means peak in Spanish. It would take a lifetime to get acquainted with all the mountains, mounts, buttes, mesas, ridges, rincons, plateaus, spires, spears and picachos.

You might want to start with Silly Mountain, at the foot of the Superstitions near Apache Junction, and work your way up.

9 – SOMETIMES THE NAME IS THE MOST INTERESTING THING ABOUT A PLACE

In the hilly Sycamore Basin country of central Arizona, a tributary of the Verde River was long labeled "Taul Creek" on maps. Then map makers for the U.S. Geological Survey heard the story behind its name:

About 1905, a cowboy named Charlie Wingfield was cleaning up in the creek so he could go to a rodeo in Camp Verde.

He lost his towel in the creek, and complained bitterly in cowboy dialect about losing his "taul." The U.S.G.S. has since renamed the stream Towel Creek.

There's a continuing fascination with some of the unlikely names of Arizona places. Take The Gap, a trading post and a cluster of dwellings alongside U.S. 89 north of Flagstaff, on the western end of the Navajo Indian Reservation. The Gap has no connection with the casual clothing chain by the same name. However, the trading post at The Gap has long been an outlet for Levi's jeans.

It is named because just to the east of the community, there is a gap in the beautiful Echo Cliffs which parallel the highway.

Here are some other yarns about how Arizona places were named:

HAPPY JACK: I take this one personally. In 1946 my father was one of the founding fathers of Happy Jack, forty-five miles southeast of Flagstaff on the road to Long Valley and the Mogollon Rim.

There was a large logging town on one side of the road, and a fair-size Forest Service facility on the other. The supervisor of the Coconino National Forest named it Happy Jack, after a location in Wyoming.

Happy Jack thrived for thirty years. Then the logging camp moved fifteen miles down the road to a place near Long Valley. The Happy Jack post office was relocated to Long Valley itself, near a place called Clints Well.

Today, few know the original location of Happy Jack. Many think of Long Valley, and the summer home subdivisions for miles around, as being Happy Jack.

To further complicate matters, the Forest Service station at the original Happy Jack has been renamed Long Valley Ranger Station. There's no accounting for bureaucracy.

PHOENIX: Phoenix rose on the site of villages once occupied by the vanished Hohokam. Thus the city was named for the mythical bird which rose from its own ashes.

Adventurer Jack Swilling formed a ditch company and began copying the Hohokam irrigation canals in 1867. As with all things historical, there is some squabbling over who named the place: Swilling or a member of his ditch company, or an educated English expatriate named Darrel Duppa.

The smart money says Swilling applied the name Phoenix to his original settlement, near present-day Sky Harbor International Airport. Duppa applied it to the new town site, surveyed in 1870 three miles west of Swilling's hamlet. (Duppa is credited with naming nearby Tempe for the Vale of Tempe in Greece.)

FLAGSTAFF: On July 4, 1876, when America was celebrating its centennial, a party of immigrants from Boston camped near the west end of present-day Flagstaff. They stripped the limbs from a tall pine tree and hoisted the U.S. flag. A few years later, when the Atlantic & Pacific Railroad was built through northern Arizona, Flagstaff became a booming lumbering and ranching town.

TOMBSTONE: Ed Schieffelin, a wandering prospector, got a chance in 1877 to go into southeastern Arizona in the company of soldiers. That was a good way to go, because Chiricahua Apaches in the region resented the white man.

Camped at Camp Huachuca, Schieffelin began eyeing some low mountains to the northeast. Dan O'Leary, a civilian scout for the army, warned Schieffelin that if he went prospecting alone, he would find only his tombstone. When Schieffelin evaded Indians and found a rich silver mine, he called it the Tombstone. A Hollywood press agent couldn't have done better. Tombstone became a rip-roaring town, made famous by the Gunfight at OK Corral. Its long-lived newspaper, *The Epitaph,* is still published in local and national editions.

SHOW LOW: Corydon E. Cooley was a government scout and deputy sheriff in eastern Arizona during the 1870s and 1880s. He married the daughter of Chief Pedro of the White Mountain Apaches.

One of his many ventures was a ranch he operated with his partner, Marion Clark. They started a store and small settlement, but couldn't get along. They agreed to play a game of lowball poker to see who would leave the ranch. As the game reached its climax, Clark told Cooley, "If you can show low, you win."

Cooley lay down his low-ball hand, including the deuce of clubs, and said, "Show Low it is." Show Low is a thriving small city today; its main street is Deuce of Clubs Avenue.

SNOWFLAKE: This town has nothing to do with weather. The Mormon settlement was founded by pioneer William J. Flake at the behest of Erastus Snow, a Mormon leader in the region. Their names were combined to name their town.

TUBA CITY: This town on the Navajo Reservation is a windy place, but it has nothing to do with the big musical instrument. When Mormon colonizers tried to settle there, it was occupied by Hopis. One Hopi chief had a name that sounded like "Tuba" to the Mormons. The name stuck.

CORNVILLE: When the post office was established in 1885, settlers in this Verde Valley community wanted to name it Coneville for a pioneer family named Cone. Papers came back from Washington listing the place as Cornville, and thus it has been to this day.

10 – THE LAST COWBOY HASN'T BEEN BORN YET

Back in 1895, James H. McClintock, a printer and later well-known Arizona historian, wrote a newspaper article debunking the myth of the Arizona cowboy and predicting his demise.

A century later, the cowboy influence still permeates Arizona. While there are lots fewer cattle than there used to be, there are still quite a few ranchers and cowboys. And there are several hundred thousand people who mimic cowboy dress and mannerisms.

Now and then an author or a video producer will come up with a new look at the "last of the cowboys." They'll get some pretty good quotes from a genuine brush-hopping hired hand, who has spent his whole life learning to talk in the colorful cowboy way.

The last cowboy hasn't been born yet. His mother's still in grade school, flirting with the young guys who come into her father's feed store.

I was never a cowboy, but tried to act the part. As a teenager, I ran around northern Arizona wearing tight Levi's, pointy-toed boots with a 24/8s heel, and a flat-brimmed black hat. My friends called me "Carpet Tack." We'd go to all the cowboy dances and a rodeo now and then.

I've chased Herefords through a squeeze chute, and driven the four-wheel-drive chuck wagon, picking up the calves that got tuckered out on a cattle drive. I know how to handle a barbed-wire gate.

But my last ride on a cow pony, some thirty-five years ago, is better forgotten. I'm a devout city dweller, as are many who pretend to be cowboys. They have been right at home since the urban cowboy craze of the 1970s.

Sometimes it's hard to tell the real thing from the Saturday night cowboys, because the genuine article frequently wears Reeboks and a John Deere cap. The boots and Stetson are reserved for ceremonial occasions, like a bull sale or jury duty.

A practiced eye will pick up a real cowboy by his leather skin and eyes that have faded from being out in the sun too long. He walks as though he just got out of the hospital. Only rodeo cowboys swagger, and that is most likely a manifestation of fear.

A true cowboy never removes his hat unless he is in bed or in church. And there's something about the way a cowboy handles his cigarette. The Englishmen holds his cigarette between thumb and forefinger, as though it were a classroom pointer. The cowboy holds his between thumb and middle finger, turned inward toward his palm, as thought it was something nasty and he was trying to figure out where to ditch it. Many cowboys have switched to chewing snuff, and the little round cans have made permanent marks in the left hip pockets of their jeans. Some city women have been awed when they mistook the little cans as condom containers.

Here are some insights into the genuine cowboy culture:

RANCHING: The federal government and environmentalists seem determined to drive the cowman off public land in the West, where ranches are already dwindling. The rancher is beset by high land prices, regulations, inflation, taxes, weather and the volatile beef market. He will be happy to complain to you, in infinite detail.

Some big ranches are now owned by people who made a fortune in some other line of work and are willing to sink their riches into an expensive lifestyle; or by a genuine rancher who inherited the ranch from his father. One leathery old-timer bought a lottery ticket and someone asked what he'd do if he won the lottery. He replied, "Oh, I'll just keep ranching until

49

the money's all gone."

NUMBERS: Never ask a rancher how many cattle he owns, or how many he sold at the auction. That is very impolite. He many not want the Forest Service or IRS to know how many head he runs. However, he will be happy to tell you how low cattle prices are and how he should have sold last spring.

REAL COWBOYS: It is not yet possible to raise a cow entirely by computer. Therefore, someone has to fix fence, haul feed, brand calves, fix pumps and windmills, read weather and grass, and haul the boss's cadillac out of a mudhole. It is still necessary to saddle up and ride into the brush to gather cattle.

If this person is a hired hand or a rancher's son (or daughter) he or she is a legitimate cowperson. These are usually very young or very old; sometimes they hold outside jobs, such as working seasonally for the hated Forest Service.

PART-TIME COWBOYS: A rancher's children, wife, nieces and nephews or romantic friends—anyone who can be counted on or bribed when it's time to ship cattle, or when there's a bad storm so you have to haul feed to the cattle.

PHANTOM COWBOYS: You have to go into the rugged Bloody Basin country or the wilds of Yavapai County to encounter these men. They may be undocumented aliens, or Native Americans who don't like city life. Or they may be whites whose wives' divorce attorneys are after them for child support.

ROPERS: These may not be working cowboys. They may be doctors or miners or firemen or drywall contractors who can afford horses, trailers, pickup trucks and charitable contributions called "entry fees." They spend their weekends on the road, competing for prize money at jackpot ropings.

RODEO COWBOYS: Any of the above who thinks he is

good enough to travel in search of big money, fame and romance. Their skills are usually too sharply honed to be useful on a ranch. Arizona has produced several national champions.

COWBOY BARS: Some of the most picturesque and democratic establishments in Arizona. Usually staffed by a country-western band. Dudes are welcome, but pacifists and gun opponents are not.

COWBOYS AND INDIANS: Many Indians are cowboys, and dress like cowboys. However, a cowboy rarely dresses like an Indian.

GATES: Always leave gates the way you found them— usually closed, so the cows don't wander off the ranch. Cattle are not very smart about geography. If you're riding in a pickup cab, try to ride in the middle so you don't have to get out and wrestle a barbed-wire gate and make a fool of yourself.

11 – BEWARE OF THE INDIAN EXPERTS

There are nearly 200,000 Native Americans in Arizona, not counting roughly half a million people who claim some percentage of Cherokee blood.

I was giving a talk about Arizona to a group of senior citizens when one wizened gentleman asked, "Do you think the Indians will ever amount to anything?"

Now, I'm not an "Indian expert." I was an expert for a few months one time, until I discovered how little I knew about the varied Indian cultures in Arizona. But many of us who have lived here a long time have been made more sensitive to Indian beliefs than our ancestors were.

With the zeal of a convert, I told the man: "If you're asking if the Indians will embrace the values you lived by back in Jersey City, no, they won't amount to much. But if you mean will they live according to the values of their own cultures, which worked fine for them before we came along, they're already doing pretty well."

The man persisted, "Aren't they a bunch of communists?"

"Sometimes they live in communal ways," I answered, "giving up personal ambition for the good of their families or clans. But I wouldn't say they were communists."

The irony of the exchange was that it occurred at a time when Native Americans were asserting themselves in a number of ways—demanding that white men return the bones of their ancestors, taken in the name of "research;" changing the names of their tribes and their towns back to their native tongue. My point is that there are a lot of Native Americans on Arizona's twenty reservations, and if you take the time to learn how their thinking differs from ours, you'll be richer for it.

It is a mistake to think Native Americans are a monolithic group. Some are Democrats and some Republicans; some follow their ancestral spiritual beliefs, others have converted to Christianity, and still others take the best of both brands of "religion." Many Arizonan Indians have intermarried with members of other tribes, or have white or Hispanic spouses.

Beware of those who claim to be "Indian experts," whether they be white or Native American. Most self-proclaimed experts are full-blooded mythologists.

Indians have been coerced, ignored, displaced, plundered, exploited, urbanized, studied, analyzed and lied to. Yet native cultures have endured in the Southwest as nowhere else.

A reservation has a stronger hold on its people than does the average white person's hometown. An urban Native American may have multiple degrees, a good job and a cellular phone. But every so often he has to return to the reservation to get in touch with his spirituality. He needs to get away from Anglos' frantic, competitive thinking and seek the understanding of blood kin who regard time and achievement differently.

The largest reservation is that of the Navajo Nation, which fills the northeastern corner of Arizona and spills over into New Mexico and Utah. Navajos refer to themselves as "Dineh," the people, and to their land as "Dinetah." They also call it "the big Rez." Their domain is as large as West Virginia and supports a population estimated at nearly a quarter million people.

As with other reservations, you're welcome to visit this one, with its vast scenic views and a glimpse of traditional Navajo life. But remember that it is someone's ancestral land, not Six Flags. Many reservations welcome outsiders during tribal fairs, and some have cultural centers to help non-Indians understand more of the native history and culture.

Within the Navajo Reservation lies the Hopi Reservation, and that's sometimes a touchy subject. The Hopis, descendants of ancient Pueblo peoples, and the Navajos, newer Athapascan arrivals, have never been great friends. They have been engaged in complicated land disputes for many years.

One Hopi village, Oraibi, may be the oldest continuously inhabited community in the United States, dating back to about

1050 A.D. The Hopis have reclaimed their historic name Kykotsmovi for their tribal capital. Whites used to call it New Oraibi.

Another of Arizona's large tribes, long known as the Papagos, have taken back their own name for themselves: Tohono O'odham. Their main reservation is along the Mexican border west and south of Tucson.

The Tohono O'odham and their blood kin, the Pima and Maricopa peoples (all thought to have descended from the vanished Hohokam) were the first Indians to be contacted by Spanish missionaries and soldiers in the 1500s. More than four hundred years of "civilization" has altered the Tohono O'odham culture, but not greatly influenced the people to act like whites.

Pimas and Maricopas live closer to town, on the Gila River Reservation between Phoenix and Tucson, and the Salt River Reservation east of Scottsdale. The Pimas helped supply early Anglo arrivals with wheat and vegetables, and helped fight a mutual enemy, the Apache.

Apaches won a good deal of notoriety in the last century for the guerilla warfare by which they defended their land. Today two Apache tribes occupy a good deal of eastern Arizona. White Mountain Apaches have worked to develop their forested Fort Apache Reservation into an appealing place for outdoor tourists. They have built many lakes and a ski resort, and created campgrounds along beautiful trout streams. Immediately to the south, San Carlos Apaches live on the San Carlos Reservation, primarily cattle ranching country and some lumbering.

One tribe, the Havasupais, have had perhaps more visitors per capita than any other native group. A few hundred Havasupais live in the remote village of Supai in Havasu Canyon, a tributary to the Colorado River in the depths of the Grand

Canyon. Supai can only be reached by foot, horseback or helicopter. It is often called "Arizona's Shangri-la." Because it's so hard to visit Supai, almost everyone wants to.

Cocopahs, Chemehuevis (formerly called "Yumas" by Anglos) and Mohaves live near the Colorado River in western Arizona. The Hualapai tribe controls the south side of the Colorado River west of the Grand Canyon, totaling not quite a million acres of grazing land and rugged canyons. Up in the Arizona Strip, north of the Grand Canyon and adjacent to the Utah border, a couple of hundred Paiutes live on the Kaibab reservation.

Members of the Yavapai tribe live on small reservations at Fort McDowell, Campe Verde, Prescott and Payson. Early Anglos often mistook the Yavapais for Apaches, and Yavapais have worked for years to set the record straight.

There is also a Tucson reservation for Yaquis, Mexican Indians who fled to Arizona around the turn of the century to avoid persecution by one Mexican government or another. Yaquis traditionally lived in small enclaves in Tucson and Scottsdale, and in their own town, Guadalupe, near Tempe. Being Mexican Indians, they were not federally recognized until 1964, when Congress set aside a 202-acre Yaqui reservation near Tucson.

In 1990, a small northern Arizona band called the San Juan Paiutes, who had been hanging out with the Navajos, were federally recognized as the nation's 509th Indian tribe.

12 – FORT PHOENIX AND OTHER INSIDE STORIES

No doubt there are regional rivalries where you come from. But you have never experienced anything like the hostility aimed at Phoenix and Maricopa County by residents of the other fourteen counties.

This hostility, based largely on envy, dates back to at least 1885, when the Thirteenth Territorial Legislature, nicknamed "The Thieving Thirteenth," distributed patronage spoils. Phoenix got $100,000 to establish the insane asylum, which provided a number of patronage jobs, and nearby Tempe got $50,000 to establish the Normal School (a college for teachers), now Arizona State University. Yuma was allowed to keep the territorial prison.

Tucson, largest city in the state at that time, was stuck with $25,000 to establish the University of Arizona. The senator from Pima County (Tucson) was pelted with rotting fruit when he tried to explain in Tucson why he had been forced to knuckle under to the greedy Phoenix crowd and settle for a university.

Phoenix, which had the Arizona Canal and a new railroad to help boost the town's growth, realized that the Capitol would be a much greater patronage plum. In 1889, Maricopa County called in (or bought) enough favors to move the Capitol to Phoenix. (The Capitol had been in Prescott originally, moved to Tucson for 10 years, then back to Prescott.)

A Prescott editor was angry at greedy Phoenix for selfishly "reaching after the earth and the balance of the universe."

While dislike of the metropolitan area is distributed throughout the state, feelings are most intense in Tucson. Between the 1910 census and the 1920 census, Phoenix surpassed Tucson in population. Since then, Phoenix has gotten increasingly larger, and Tucson has gotten branch offices.

There is a deadly, intense rivalry between the two cities, but only Tucson knows that the rivalry exists. Phoenix could care less. There is a strange contradiction in Tucson's attitude. Residents of that city consider Tucson a superior place to live, a cultured Athens of Arizona. They may be right. Yet Tucsonans seem to envy Phoenix the very economic and political engines they claim have made the capital city unlivable.

WHY ALL THE FUSS OVER OSTRICHES?

Sometimes when ostriches are mentioned, you'll see a flicker of recognition on those well-versed in the lore of Arizona. And you may wonder why suburban Chandler has an annual ostrich festival.

Before the turn of the century, a developer, farmer and merchant named Josiah N. Harbert introduced ostriches into the valley. Soon, many ostrich ranches helped supply the needs of women around the world who desired ostrich plumes to finish off their costumes. Sometimes ostriches and their eggs were eaten, but the birds were usually considered more valuable for their plumes; a male bird was worth $1,000.

Around the time World War I began, fashion veered away from the plumes. And the war in Europe put a kink in international commerce. Soon surplus ostriches were being sold for $10 a head. A flock of three hundred ostriches being herded cattle-drive style from west of Phoenix to Chandler stampeded, upsetting the buggy occupied by a farm couple and killing the woman.

In that same year, 1914, the government contracted for 25,000 pounds of Arizona ostrich meat to supplement the diets of civilians, so that beef and pork could be shipped to troops in France.

Eighty years later, ostrich-growing was again beginning to thrive in Arizona. While the boom was fueled in part by promoters who delighted in selling breeding stock to the unwary for upwards of $25,000 a bird, ostrich skin was much in demand for boots and shoes, and there was a growing market for ostrich meat.

SO, WHAT ABOUT THE CAMELS?

Beginning in 1851, several government exploration parties crossed Arizona from east to west, seeking to establish a railroad route near the thirty-fifth parallel (roughly where the Santa Fe mainline and Interstate 40 now go).

In 1857, Lt. Edward F. Beale was assigned to build a wagon road along the thirty-fifth parallel. Beale was a dashing Navy officer who had attracted attention in Washington by smuggling himself through hostile Mexico to bring the first word to the eastern United States of the gold strike at Sutter's Mill in California.

The Army was experimenting with camels as beasts of burden. The scheme was the pet of Secretary of War Jefferson Davis (later president of the Confederacy), who hoped camels would be more durable and cost-efficient than mules. Beale started out from Texas with an assortment of animals, including two dozen camels. Beale rode a white dromedary, and when he got saddle-sore, he rode in a bright red Army ambulance.

Beale crossed Arizona, reached the Pacific and rested north of Los Angeles. On the return trip, he accidentally met up with the pioneer steamship *General Jessup,* exploring the Colorado River not far from present-day Hoover Dam. The boat hauled twenty camels across the river for Beale.

Beale made another trip in 1859, again using camels. He was sold on the practicality of the ungainly beasts, but others found them smelly, mean, and upsetting to horses and mules.

The Civil War put an end to the camel experiment. But some of the army's camels remained in the Southwest until the early 1900s. So did a colorful Persian camel driver named Hadji Alli, one of Beale's imported camel jockeys. His American nickname was "Hi Jolly." Hi Jolly is buried at Quartzsite, Arizona, near the Colorado River.

THE BARON OF ARIZONA

James Addison Reavis was a St. Louis trolley motorman, and a formidable con man. Over a period of years, he married a young Hispanic orphan from California, created fictional pasts for them both, and invented a Spanish land grant in the name of the Peralta family of Spain. Reavis' wife, of course, was the last natural heir to the grant. By this time he was working in Arizona as circulation agent for a San Francisco newspaper.

Reavis traveled to Spain and Mexico to plant fictitious documents in their archives. Finally, in 1883, he introduced the land grant into federal courts, claiming a huge chunk of central Arizona. The grant included the sites of Phoenix and its suburbs, and several mining towns between Phoenix and Silver City, New Mexico.

The grants withstood rigorous inspection for years. The Southern Pacific Railroad, Silver King Mine and many lesser landowners paid Reavis for the right to their own property.

Reavis was unmasked in 1890; five years later the courts officially declared his grant a fraud, and sent him to prison for a couple of years. He was soon back on the streets, hustling other fast-buck schemes.

LOST MINES AND TREASURES

Stories of mislaid mines and buried treasure are so prevalent and complex that we don't have room to even sketch them here. Volumes have been written about these mines, including the biggest and most appealing fraud of all, the Lost Dutchman.

The author has made more money writing about lost mines than others have made looking for gold. But the treasure hunters probably had more fun.

13 – WHAT YOU COULD HAVE BOUGHT ARIZONA FOR IF ONLY YOU HAD ARRIVED EARLIER

A former state land commissioner used to boast, "I'm one of those natives who was too smart to invest in Arizona land."

Many long-time Arizonans measure their tenure here by comparing what they could have bought land for when they arrived: "You could buy that desert land for $15 dollars an acre when I came here in 1952." Of course, in 1952 you needed $15 to pay the gas and phone bills.

It's a status game. Those quaint adventurers who arrived before World War II have an edge over those who joined the stampede after the war.

We natives have the greatest edge, plus the dubious distinction of lacking the vision to capitalize on Arizona's rapid growth. Most of us left making money to immigrants from New Jersey, who recognized the potential to make a lot of money by providing housing for all the people who were building homes. Even those natives who inherited land were caught unawares as the family farm was purchased and planted with houses and condos.

Just the other day, a woman phoned to tell me how her father brought her here from Ohio in 1944, so she wouldn't die of asthma. As she grew up here, she marveled at the high prices people were asking for land in Paradise Valley: $500 an acre. Who wanted it? Since then, the city of Phoenix has burst through passes in the Phoenix Mountains, filled Paradise Valley with homes and swept on northward to Deer Valley.

In 1945, my parents bought a house and two vacant lots in the village of Camp Verde for $500. Three years later they sold the property for $800. I'd guess it's worth $100,000 today.

Jeweler and philanthropist Newt Rosenzweig likes to tell how he and his brother Harry joined up with contractor Del Webb to build high rise buildings on residential property his father had bought in the 1920s. That was way out on Central Avenue in Phoenix, almost to Indian School Road. His mother wouldn't live there because it was too far out of town to have natural gas piped in.

Now the former Rosenzweig Center is considered to be in central Phoenix. That's another part of this story—trying to remember where the city limits, and lots of landmarks, used to be.

"You're a native?" the visitor asks incredulously. "I'll bet you've seen a lot of changes."

Not necessarily. Unless you're patrolling the vast Salt River Valley daily, you don't actually see the changes. For the first time in a couple of years, you drive down what used to be a rural farm road. You can't recognize the urban scene you now encounter.

I only recently located the urban enclave called Weedville, where my ancestors lived briefly when they came to Arizona in 1917. It is wrapped in the arms of the sprawling city of Peoria, a tiny town when I was born.

A few years later, we lived way out in the country, where the southbound access road now enters Interstate 17 at Northern Avenue. My mother used to send me up a dusty lane to buy eggs from Mrs. Roer, a widow. Her son Bill says her farm house was "an eighth of a mile north of Northern in the high-speed lane (of today's busy freeway)."

Just west of the present freeway site was a field where my brother and I played. It has since lived one life as the site of a drive-in theater, and for at least a generation has been the home of a K-Mart store and a coffee shop. It's about time to tear them down and build something new.

Bill Roer and I remember when the Valley's north-south

thoroughfares were called "laterals," identified by the number of the adjacent irrigation ditches than ran south from the Arizona Canal.

Roer's childhood home was between Lateral 13 (now 19th Avenue) and Lateral 14 (27th Avenue), also known then as Mission Drive, for the Mission Dairy at what is now 27th Avenue and Camelback. Not far to the west, some Glendale old-timers still call 59th Avenue simply "Eighteen."

There's still time to play this game. To get in on the action, drive to the perimeter of the town where you're living, if you can afford that much gasoline.

Take a good look. You can even take notes if you like. Then go back in two years and try to find the place.

14 - POLITICS MAKES STRANGE BED BUGS

Arizona has tried to maintain an air of rugged individualism, to be a place were truly independent people can live out their beliefs and lifestyle free of government meddling.

Former U.S. Senator Barry Goldwater became the guru of this philosophy. After he lost the 1964 presidential election to Lyndon B. Johnson, he retained his credibility by periodically changing his mind.

In fact, however, Arizona has relied heavily on federal money of one sort or another since the 1850s. The closing of a frontier cavalry post was as hotly decried in the 1870s as was the closing of Williams Air Force Base in the 1990s.

It is but one of the many contradictions in Arizona's picturesque politics.

When Arizona became a state in 1912, it established a bicameral legislature: a Senate and a House of Representatives to oversee Special Interest Groups, then known as "lobbies."

Until the 1960s, outlying counties had equal representation with the rural counties, Pima and Maricopa. Of the outlying counties, none could out lie Gila County, where many people didn't vote until after they were dead.

Large special interest groups, mainly the copper industry, found it easy to purchase legislative loyalty in these rural counties. It was said that Arizona wore "the copper collar."

The Legislature was dominated by "pinto" Democrats—democratic on social issues, but fiscal conservatives.

All that ended in the 1960s, with the one-man, one-vote rulings of the U.S. Supreme Court. Not only did Maricopa and Pima Counties get more legislative votes; thousands of Republicans had moved here from Indiana, making this a true two-party state. Since then, urban special interest groups are in the saddle.

Periodically, newspapers and county attorneys discover a nest of corruption in state government. One of the more recent scandals was the "AZscam" sting operation in the 1990s, when several politicians went to jail for accepting bribes to vote for legalized gambling. A couple of government reorganizations came out of these crusades, and officeholders and entrenched functionaries had to quickly figure out how to work around them. In Arizona, as elsewhere, the first obligation of a state agency is to perpetuate itself.

Government really started getting quirky in 1988. Governor Bruce Babbitt had decided to seek the Democratic nomination for president.

In a squirrely three-way gubernatorial campaign which split Democrats two ways, Arizonans replaced Babbitt with Republican Evan Mecham, who had sought the governorship for years. Two years later, Mecham was impeached.

He was succeeded by another wannabe governor, long-time Secretary of State Rose Mofford. Arizona's first woman governor served the rest of that term and decided she didn't really like the job.

In the election that followed, neither Democrat Terry Goddard nor Republican Fife Symington got a clear majority,

67

required by a kinky state law that had slipped past the Legislature. Symington won the runoff and was still governor in 1996, when the federal government indicted him on twenty-six counts of fraud in connection with his business dealings before he was governor.

While in office, Mecham had rescinded Babbitt's executive order declaring a holiday in honor of Martin Luther King Jr. That stirred up an international crisis, and resulting charges of racism hurt the state's tourist business. The National Football League pulled the 1993 Super Bowl out of Phoenix.

Arizona voters finally approved the King holiday. This is one of the few states where voters had a chance to vote on the holiday.

Early in 1994, Babbitt appeared to be President Clinton's choice to replace Harry Blackmun on the U.S. Supreme Court. Clinton changed his mind, possibly because Arizona already had more than its share of Supreme Court justices: Chief Justice William H. Rehnquist and Sandra Day O'Connor, the first woman justice in the court's history.

Go figure it.

Until you get acquainted with Arizona politics, you need to join a special interest group and hang on.

15 - IT'S TIME YOU LEARNED ABOUT THIS

The Navajo Reservation extends about halfway across the top of Northern Arizona, and the Hopi Reservation lies entirely with the Navajo boundaries. The two tribes use three different time zones: Mountain Standard, Mountain Daylight and Indian Time.

The enchanted clockwork doesn't end at the reservation borders. At a tavern in the Arizona strip, happy hour begins in mid-afternoon. Half a mile away in Utah, where liquor laws are weird, the clocks run an hour faster in summer, so drinkers like to come over to Arizona.

Arizona has never liked the idea of daylight savings time. The state tried it a couple of times. We already have more daylight than we can use. Natives argue that if God had wanted them to save daylight, he'd have made the nights longer. Besides, parts of western Arizona were beyond what should be the western boundary of the Pacific Time Zone. Street lights hardly come on before working people in Yuma and Kingman have to be in bed.

So the state voted itself out of the Uniform Time Act, which went into effect in 1967. Arizona refused to adopt DST in April and return to standard time in October, joining such elite places as Hawaii and American Samoa in sticking to standard time year-round.

This causes some consternation for those who have business with the East Coast. Your contact there will be out to lunch by the time you get to work. From April to October you need to check airline schedules very carefully. The airlines always seem to get it right, but you may miscalculate.

If Indian Time sounds like a racial slur, it is not. The phrase was coined by Native Americans, and expresses their humorous approach to the white man's rigid time constraints.

Basically, the concept is that in this complex world, clock time is the least important element. If a thing is worth doing, time will be made for it. This applies to a visit with a friend, or communing with nature, or telling a story. One Native American who collects Indian stories told me, "When an Indian begins a story, he starts with a leaf falling from a tree and floating down the stream . . . and floating and floating. It took me three days to gather some of these stories."

Under the Uniform Time Act, the Navajo Nation opted to go with daylight savings. The Hopis decided to stay on Mountain Standard Time, like the rest of Arizona. If you have an appointment in the Hopi capital of Kykotsmovi, remember to set your watch ahead an hour as you enter the Navajo Reservation. Then set your watch back an hour as you cross the Hopi boundary.

Then put your watch in the glove box, because you'll be operating on Indian time anyway.

16 – MORE COMPLICATED THAN JERKY AND SUN TEA

One of the first things you'll run into on a get-acquainted visit to Arizona is the so-called cowboy steak. It is a large cut of beef, frequently marinated for tenderness, served on a platter with pinto beans and bread and, if you're really lucky, some kind of salad.

These are served in rustic, barn-like places with phony ghost-town decor. In some places, daring customers wear neckties just so the waitresses can cut them off and staple them to the wall. If you order your steak well done, you may get an old cowboy boot served on your platter as a gag.

These cowboy steak houses are authentic in the sense that (1) beef on the hoof was often the handiest thing to the chuck wagon (2) they are frequented by a few real cowboys whose tastes in food are not sophisticated; some of them figure Mexican food is indigenous, and the only ethnic food they know is Swiss steak.

A genuine cowboy steak would more likely be round steak, tenderized with a claw hammer, floured and fried in lard. A rancher couldn't afford to feed the hired hands T-bones, which he could sell on the hoof to people willing to pay more for them.

The cuisine of Arizona and the Southwest has gotten a lot more sophisticated in recent decades. There are more Thai restaurants than Mexican. Five-star restaurants and gourmet food stores have sprung up in the metropolitan areas. Recreational cooks blend the best parts of the world's cooking for luncheons and dinner parties.

However, Arizona cuisine is rooted in certain homey traditions you need to be aware of. Let's begin with the tall tales and work our way forward:

Many people think that Miller Brewing Company invented

light (or Lite) beer. Light beer was actually invented in Arizona during Prohibition. Bottleggers in an out-of-the-way hamlet were busy supplying the needs of thirsty city-dwellers—until a drought dried up the spring.

The resourceful bootleggers simply located a mirage, an image of a mountain lake surrounded by pine trees. They then siphoned water from the lake to make the world's first light beer.

A little later, dehydrated water was invented in Pinal County, to reduce the cost of pumping water from Arizona's falling ground water table. Ranchers found out that cattle grown with dehydrated water allowed them to bypass the middle man. Instead of selling to a packing plant, a rancher could slice up his beef and sell it directly to bar owners as jerky. (Jerky is close kin to machaca, an ingredient in some Mexican dishes.)

Most of us who grew up here liked a certain kind of Mexican fiesta food that commonly was served in Hispanic homes that had been converted to restaurants—red and green chili burros, tacos, tamales and enchiladas. You can still find that kind of food, both in the cities and in the remote towns.

What you can't find is any two people who agree on what good Mexican food is. Tex-Mex is not really popular here, nor are some of the exotic California concoctions, such as thrasher shark tacos drowned in tomato sauce.

A lighter brand of Mexican fare has become almost indigenous to the Phoenix restaurant scene. It employs less beef and less grease, and more chicken, seafood, veggies and light oils.

You can still find restaurants in the metropolitan area which serve hot Mexican food. This stuff will clear your sinuses and make your hair sweat, but the heat tends to obliterate the more savory flavors of good red or green chili.

Traditions endure. At a New Year's Day roping contest near Globe, Hispanic cowboys kept calling plaintively to the chuck wagon cook, "Is the menudo done yet?" Menudo, a soup containing tripe, hominy and cilantro, is reputed to cure hangovers.

Once, on the Navajo Reservation, I was the guest of a tribal official who promised to buy me a real Navajo lunch. That turned out to be a cup of coffee and a slice of greasy fry bread. I like fry bread, a delicacy when it's served with chili or honey or beans. But that dry chunk of fry bread barely got me through until dinner time.

There is some confusion between Indian fry bread and Mexican sopaipillas, which are almost interchangeable. Sopaipillas tend to be lighter (except when I make them), and they make a nice dessert when served with powdered sugar or butter and honey.

Fry bread is employed to make a delicious Navajo taco. This dish originated on the Navajo Reservation and has spread throughout the state. It is simply a large round of fry bread embellished with red or green chili con carne, and the other accouterments of traditional Spanish food—shredded cheese, chopped tomatoes, shredded lettuce.

Beef has always been a mainstay. The Arizona Cattlegrowers Association and its gung-ho auxiliary, the Arizona Cowbelles, promoted beef so enthusiastically that I was tempted to write *The Beef is Boring Cookbook.*

Nowadays I feel a little sorry for the beef lobby. Health-conscious Arizonans have switched to chicken breasts, turkey hotdogs and fish tacos.

Maybe the cowboy steaks and pinto beans aren't such a bad deal after all.

FINAL EXAM TIME

This is your final examination for *Arizona 101*. It is the same test used by the Commission on Arizona Citizenship to naturalize newcomers.

Do not look at your neighbor's paper. When you have completed the exam, put it into an envelope and mail it to your nearest relative or closest friend back home. Do not send it to the instructor for *Arizona 101*. He is looking forward to a vacation at his favorite unspoiled (Arizona) (there are a few left) spots. He neglected to tell you about that hideaway, didn't he? Too bad.

1. The southern part of Arizona was made part of the United States by the:
    A. Volstead Act
    B. Gadsen Purchase
    C. Treaty of Guadalupe Jimenez

2. For more than a decade, Arizona was part of this territory:
    A. New Mexico
    B. Deseret
    C. Nevada

3. February 14, 1912, is celebrated in Arizona because:
    A. It was the first Valentine's day
    B. It was the day knives and forks were introduced in Tucson
    C. It is Arizona Statehood Day

4. The area where Las Vegas is now located once belonged to Arizona and was called:
   A. Pah-Ute County
   B. Sierra Madre
   C. Peyote County

5. The oldest continuously inhabited community in Arizona (and maybe in North America) is:
   A. Sun City
   B. Oraibi
   C. Tucson

6. The word "Hohokam" means:
   A. Laughing Boy
   B. Those who have gone
   C. An economical Japanese pickup

7. The Arizona Strip is :
   A. An exotic dance
   B. A cut of beef steak
   C. The part of Arizona north of the Colorado River

8. The Mogollon Rim separates:
   A. Mongolia and Manchuria
   B. Mohave and Yavapai Counties
   C. The river systems of the Colorado and Gila rivers

9. If Rancher John had 475 head of cattle and sold twelve percent of them at auction, the estimated population of Arizona would be:
   A. 4 million
   B. 6.7 million
   C. Anybody's guess

10. Black River and White River rise in eastern Arizona and join to form the:
    A. Gray River
    B. Salt River
    C. Little Pecos River

11. A majority of Arizonans:
    A. Were born here
    B. Weren't born here
    C. Haven't moved here yet

12. Arizona's population density is
    A. 35 people per square mile
    B. 1.2 people per square mile
    C. Arizonans are denser than Alaskans, not as dense as Hoosiers

13. The highest temperature ever recorded in Arizona was
    A. 148
    B. 127
    C. 118

14. The most tiresome statement heard in Arizona is "It's a dry . . .":
    A. River
    B. Martini
    C. Heat

15. "We don't care how they do it in L.A." is:
    A. The motto of the Phoenix Suns
    B. A rallying cry of Arizona natives
    C. The city motto of San Francisco

16. The Central Arizona Project is:
    A. An effort to organize migrant workers
    B. A system to bring Colorado River water to central Arizona
    C. A federally-subsidized housing development

17. Arizona's state bird is:
    A. The roadrunner
    B. The Iowa Snowbird
    C. The cactus wren

18. The Spanish word "verde" means
    A. Muddy
    B. Green
    C. Delicious

19. The largest Indian tribe in Arizona is:
    A. Navajo
    B. Tohono O'odham
    C. San Juan Paiutes

ANSWERS: 1-B; 2-A; 3-C; 4-A; 5-B; 6-B; 7-C; 8-C; 9-A; 10-B; 11-A; 12-B; 13-B; 14-C; 15-B; 16-B; 17-C; 18-B; 19-A.

FACTS AND FIGURES

Highest point in Arizona: 12,643 feet (Mt. Humphreys, north of Flagstaff)

Lowest point in Arizona: 75 feet where the Colorado River flows into Mexico south of Yuma

Highest recorded temperature: 127 degrees at Fort Mohave in 1896 and Parker in 1905

Lowest recorded temperature: -40 degrees at Hawley Lake in 1971

First European explorer: Fray Marcos de Niza, 1539

First European community: Tubac, 1852

Became part of the U.S.: North of Gila River, Treaty of Guadalupe Hidalgo, 1848; south of the Gila, Gadsden Purchase, 1854

Became Arizona Territory: February 24, 1863, President Lincoln separated Arizona from New Mexico Territory

Became forty-eighth state: February 14, 1912

State motto: Ditat Deus (God enriches)

Land area: 113,909 square miles

Geographic ranking: sixth largest state in land area

State flower: saguaro blossom

State bird: cactus wren

State tree: paloverde

State neckwear (no kidding): bola tie

State gem: turquoise

State fossil: petrified wood

State reptile: ridge-nosed rattlesnake

State mammal: ring-tail cat

State colors: blue and gold